Herein lies
the gardening
secrets of

_____

compiled
in the year

_____

Stepping

A Gardener's

Stones

Journal

Illustrations by Nicole G. Carlin

Additional copies of this book may be purchased at $16.95
(plus postage and handling) from
Hobby House Press, Inc.
1 Corporate Drive, Grantsville, MD 21536
1-800-554-1447
www.hobbyhouse.com
or from your favorite bookstore or dealer.
©2001 Hobby House Press, Inc.

Printed in the United States of America

Published by Hobby House Press
Grantsville, Maryland 21536
www.hobbyhouse.com

ISBN: 0-87588-606-X

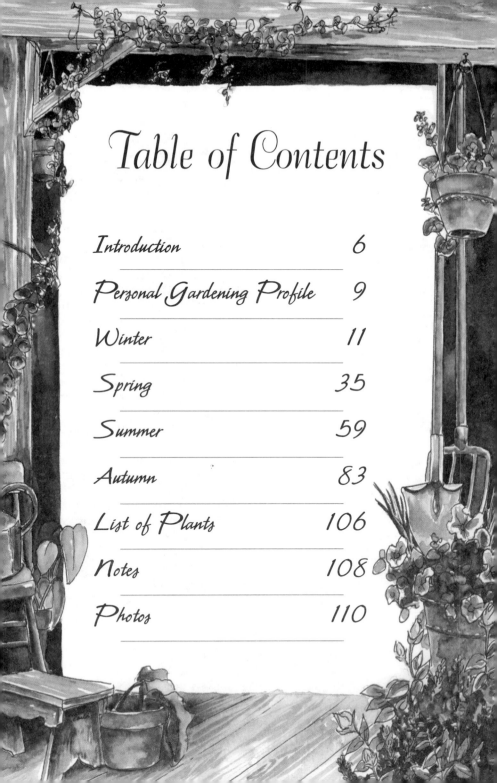

Table of Contents

Introduction

garden \gär'den\ *n* a rich well-cultivated plot of ground where herbs, fruits, flowers, or vegetables are grown

Whether it is an immaculately planned and executed English garden, a flurry of wildflowers or a humble vegetable garden, a garden will become part of your soul. It begins with a passion for growing but becomes a way of life. Perhaps it has something to do with the circle of life and how one can see this never-ending cycle season after season.

The purpose of this seasonal journal is to encourage thoughts and arouse the imagination by giving you a place to record your gardening triumphs and tragedies, observations and discoveries, secrets and questions. Perhaps you are an expert gardener with many secrets to share. Or perhaps you merely dream of the day

6

when you will have a plot of earth to cultivate. No matter what level of expertise you possess, there is always more to learn, more to discover, more to dream. This journal will prompt thought, which can only deepen your passion for this earthly delight.

Gardening is not just a summer activity. Many facets of gardening take place throughout the year. Therefore, there are four sections of this journal—one for each season. Each section begins with a poem with reference to the season. Gardening tips pertaining to the appropriate season are included throughout the pages for you to consider as you record your entries. At the end of this journal, you will find a place to list the plants you have tried and document whether they were successful or unsuccessful in your garden. Finally, there is a place for you to mount photos of your garden.

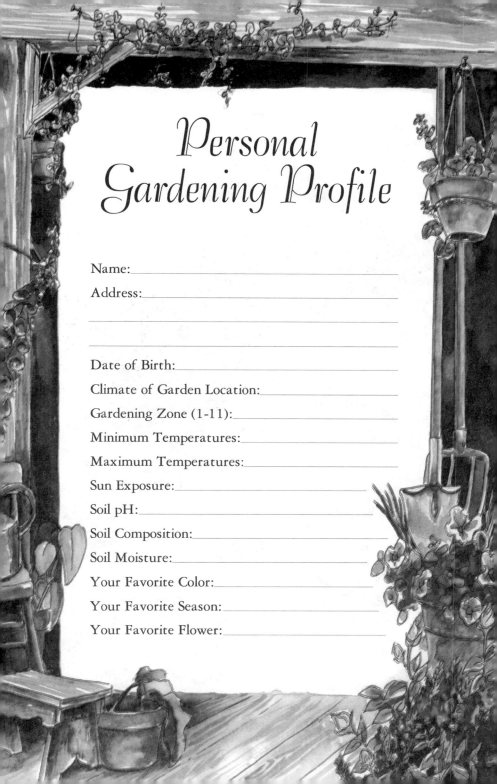

Personal
Gardening Profile

Name:_____

Address:_____

_____

_____

Date of Birth:_____

Climate of Garden Location:_____

Gardening Zone (1-11):_____

Minimum Temperatures:_____

Maximum Temperatures:_____

Sun Exposure:_____

Soil pH:_____

Soil Composition:_____

Soil Moisture:_____

Your Favorite Color:_____

Your Favorite Season:_____

Your Favorite Flower:_____

Winter

When I see birches bend to left and right
Across the lines of straighter darker trees,
I like to think some boy's been swinging them.
But swinging doesn't bend them down to stay.
Ice-storms do that. Often you must have seen them
Loaded with ice a sunny winter morning
After a rain. They click upon themselves
As the breeze rises, and turn many-colored
As the stir cracks and crazes their enamel.
Soon the sun's warmth makes them shed crystal shells
Shattering and avalanching on the snow-crust
Such heaps of broken glass to sweep away
You'd think the inner dome of heaven had fallen.
They are dragged to the withered bracken by the load,
And they seem not to break; though once they are bowed
So low for long, they never right themselves:
You may see their trunks arching in the woods
Years afterwards, trailing their leaves on the ground
Like girls on hands and knees that throw their hair
Before them over their heads to dry in the sun.

--*Birches*
by Robert Frost

Do you get snow in your garden? If so, what month does it begin to fall?

Winter Tip: Remember to feed your compost pile, turn it, and keep it moist during the winter.

$\mathcal{D}$o you plant anything special in your garden especially for the way it looks during the winter months?_____

_____

_____

_____

_____

_____

_____

_____

_____

_____

_____

_____

_____

_____

Winter Tip: Compost piles need nitrogen. Kitchen scraps are your best source in the winter, but you can also use bone meal.

What kind of wildlife takes advantage of your garden during the winter months?

_____

_____

_____

_____

_____

_____

_____

_____

_____

_____

_____

_____

_____

_____

_____

_____

_____

Winter Tip: Turn your compost pile once a month during the winter to maintain oxygen and moisture levels.

When you look at your garden during the winter months, what feelings or thoughts do you have?_____

_____

_____

_____

_____

_____

_____

_____

_____

_____

_____

_____

_____

_____

Winter Tip: Consider structure and bark when buying trees and shrubs as these factors add beauty to winter gardens.

What style did you choose for your garden?

Winter Tip: Tree guards help discourage hungry rodents and deer from stripping bark during the winter months.

Do you have a fishpond? How do you handle it during the winter months?

_____

_____

_____

_____

_____

_____

_____

_____

_____

_____

_____

_____

_____

_____

_____

Winter Tip: Stop feeding fish when the weather turns cold. They don't move as much in cold weather and therefore eat less.

What plants do you bring indoors in the winter in order to replant in the spring?

_____
_____
_____
_____
_____
_____
_____
_____
_____
_____
_____
_____
_____
_____
_____
_____

Winter Tip: A small amount of ash from fireplaces and wood-burning stoves raises pH levels of soil and supplies minerals such as calcium and potassium.

*L*ook at your outdoor garden. What shapes and colors do you see there? How do they make you feel?

_____

_____

_____

_____

_____

_____

_____

_____

_____

_____

_____

_____

_____

_____

_____

Winter Tip: Aerating your lawn in winter will allow spring fertilizer to reach the roots of your grass in spring.

Do you have a path or walkway in your garden? How do you remove any snow that accumulates on them?_____

_____

_____

_____

_____

_____

_____

_____

_____

_____

_____

_____

_____

_____

_____

_____

Winter Tip: If you live in a cold climate, fish will survive the winter outdoors if the pond is at least 2-3 feet deep.

What measures do you take prior to icy or snowy weather to prevent damage to your plants?

_____

_____

_____

_____

_____

_____

_____

_____

_____

_____

_____

_____

_____

_____

_____

Winter Tip: Pine needles lower the pH of soil, which is helpful especially in alkaline clay soil.

How do you mend plants damaged by ice or snow?

_____

_____

_____

_____

_____

_____

_____

_____

_____

_____

_____

_____

_____

_____

_____

_____

_____

_____

Winter Tip: Pine needles are great for the compost pile. Just be sure to shred them first, otherwise they will break down very slowly.

*D*o you use any plants or bushes near your house to improve the heating and cooling of your home? How?_____

_____

_____

_____

_____

_____

_____

_____

_____

_____

_____

_____

_____

_____

_____

_____

_____

Winter Tip: In winter, the view opens up in your outdoor garden—ponds, paths, and walls once concealed by plants are now focal points.

*D*o you have any water features in your garden? How do you manage them in cold weather?_____

_____

_____

_____

_____

_____

_____

_____

_____

_____

_____

_____

_____

_____

_____

_____

_____

_____

Winter Tip: To prevent a fishpond from freezing over, float a rubber ball or piece of wood on top. When ice forms, dunk the ball or wood to break the ice.

$\mathcal{D}$o you do any indoor gardening during the winter months?_____

_____

_____

_____

_____

_____

_____

_____

_____

_____

_____

_____

_____

_____

_____

_____

_____

_____

Winter Tip: Do not feed dormant houseplants.

What sounds do you notice in your garden that are specific to winter?

_____

_____

_____

_____

_____

_____

_____

_____

_____

_____

_____

_____

_____

_____

_____

_____

_____

Winter Tip: Remember to water Christmas trees especially if they are living trees. Ice cubes work well as they slowly release water into the root ball.

What are the normal high and low temperatures that you must take into consideration when planting in your garden?

_____

_____

_____

_____

_____

_____

_____

_____

_____

_____

_____

_____

_____

_____

Winter Tip: Try forcing azaleas, primula, amaryllis, paperwhite narcissus, tulips and hyacinths. Try pre-chilling them for forcing indoors.

What kind of mulch do you use on your plants to protect them from the cold temperatures during the winter months?

_____

_____

_____

_____

_____

_____

_____

_____

_____

_____

_____

_____

_____

_____

Winter Tip: Use your Christmas tree as mulch by cutting the limbs off the tree and layering them on the soil.

What was the most unusual creature that you have seen in your garden?

_____

_____

_____

_____

_____

_____

_____

_____

_____

_____

_____

_____

_____

_____

_____

_____

_____

Winter Tip: Scented geraniums, bay leaf, and rosemary are good houseplants for winter that you can also use in your kitchen.

What tips do you have for other gardeners that would help them with their winter gardening? _____

_____

_____

_____

_____

_____

_____

_____

_____

_____

_____

_____

_____

_____

_____

_____

_____

_____

_____

Winter Tip: Ornamental grasses can add height and movement to your winter garden.

What produce from your garden do you enjoy during the winter months?

_____

_____

_____

_____

_____

_____

_____

_____

_____

_____

_____

_____

_____

_____

_____

_____

_____

Winter Tip: Spread used coffee grounds on newspaper to let them dry. Then spread them around the garden.

*D*o you gather any items from your garden to decorate for the holiday season? If so, what do you collect and how do you use it?

_____

_____

_____

_____

_____

_____

_____

_____

_____

_____

_____

_____

_____

_____

_____

_____

Winter Tip: Balsam pine needles make fragrant sachets to freshen closets and drawers.

Spring

*N*ew feet within my garden go,
New fingers stir the sod;
A troubadour upon the elm
Betrays the solitude.

*N*ew children play upon the green,
New weary sleep below;
And still the pensive spring returns,
And still the punctual snow!

*P*ink, small, and punctual.
Aromatic, low,
Covert in April,
Candid in May,

*D*ear to the moss,
Known by the knoll,
Next to the robin
In every human soul.

*B*old little beauty,
Bedecked with thee,
Nature forswears
Antiquity.

--Part II: Nature LII
by Emily Dickinson

What signs of life remind you that spring is coming?

_____

_____

_____

_____

_____

_____

_____

_____

_____

_____

_____

_____

_____

_____

_____

_____

_____

Spring Tip: To re-acclimate a winterized plant, move it outside for 2 hours the first day, 4 hours the second, 6 hours the third and so on for about a week.

What bulbs have you planted for spring?

_____

_____

_____

_____

_____

_____

_____

_____

_____

_____

_____

_____

_____

_____

_____

Spring Tip: Ice storms can cause lots of damage. Remove broken limbs before buds begin to swell.

Which bulbs are you most looking forward to blooming?

_____

_____

_____

_____

_____

_____

_____

_____

_____

_____

_____

_____

_____

_____

_____

_____

_____

_____

Spring Tip: To start a new garden, cover the ground with black & white newspaper and put soil on top. The paper chokes weeds and eventually decomposes.

What part of your garden comes alive first each spring? _____

_____
_____
_____
_____
_____
_____
_____
_____
_____
_____
_____
_____
_____
_____
_____
_____

Spring Tip: When planting a vegetable garden, make sections no larger than 4 ft. wide so that every plant is within reach.

When can you begin planting seedlings or seeds into your outside garden without frost damage? _____

_____

_____

_____

_____

_____

_____

_____

_____

_____

_____

_____

_____

_____

_____

_____

_____

_____

Spring Tip: Give your hard-scape a check-up. Now is the time to repair damaged grape arbors, fences, etc.

*D*o you notice any migration patterns that bring special guests to your garden in the spring?_____

_____

_____

_____

_____

_____

_____

_____

_____

_____

_____

_____

_____

_____

_____

_____

_____

Spring Tip: Before buds emerge, spray fruit trees and ornamental shrubs with horticultural spray oil, which smothers over-wintering pests.

Where is your garden located? Would you classify it as being shady or sunny?

_____

_____

_____

_____

_____

_____

_____

_____

_____

_____

_____

_____

_____

_____

_____

_____

_____

Spring Tip: Finish pruning fruit trees while they are dormant. Rake up trimmings and run them through a chipper to add to your compost pile.

Which plant(s) took longer to sprout than you had anticipated? _____

_____

_____

_____

_____

_____

_____

_____

_____

_____

_____

_____

_____

_____

_____

_____

_____

Spring Tip: Clean your pruning tools in isopropyl alcohol between plants to prevent diseases from spreading tree to tree.

What kind of fertilizer do you give your seeds or seedlings to give them a jump-start in the spring? _____

_____

_____

_____

_____

_____

_____

_____

_____

_____

_____

_____

_____

_____

_____

Spring Tip: Stay on paths and dry patches of ground when walking through your garden. Footsteps compress wet soil crushing the tiny air pockets that help roots develop.

$\mathcal{D}$raw your garden layout.

1 cube = 1 foot

$\mathcal{D}$o you have a favorite place to buy your plants? _____

_____

_____

_____

_____

_____

_____

_____

_____

_____

_____

_____

_____

_____

_____

_____

_____

Spring Tip: Be careful when you cut back shrubs. Typically, plants that bloom in spring develop those blooms on the branches from the previous summer.

What is the most rewarding aspect of gardening?

_____
_____
_____
_____
_____
_____
_____
_____
_____
_____
_____
_____
_____
_____
_____
_____
_____
_____
_____

Spring Tip: If your roses show signs of iron deficiency (yellowing between the veins on their leaves), feed them with fertilizer containing chelated iron.

*D*o you plant mostly ornamental plants or fruits and vegetables? _____

_____

_____

_____

_____

_____

_____

_____

_____

_____

_____

_____

_____

_____

_____

_____

_____

_____

Spring Tip: Plant vegetables in pots. Cherry tomatoes, lettuce, peppers, and squash work well in pots. Keep them in your sunniest location. Water often.

$\mathcal{A}$re your flowers mostly perennials or annuals? _____

_____
_____
_____
_____
_____
_____
_____
_____
_____
_____
_____
_____
_____
_____
_____
_____
_____

Spring Tip: Light soil mix dries out quickly, so be prepared to water often – daily sometimes. Probe with your fingers beneath the surface to test.

Does your garden have a color scheme? If so, what colors do you use? Why?

_____

_____

_____

_____

_____

_____

_____

_____

_____

_____

_____

_____

_____

_____

_____

_____

_____

_____

Spring Tip: To remove pond scum from your ornamental pond, pull a piece of newspaper over the surface of the water once a week.

How do you choose which plants to put in your garden?

_____

_____

_____

_____

_____

_____

_____

_____

_____

_____

_____

_____

_____

_____

_____

_____

Spring Tip: When frequently watering potted plants, nutrients readily wash out. Regularly feed plants once or twice a month.

When you shop for plants, what signs do you look for that tell you a plant is healthy or not?

_____

_____

_____

_____

_____

_____

_____

_____

_____

_____

_____

_____

_____

_____

_____

_____

Spring Tip: Give lawns their first feeding. Provide shrubs, trees, and ground covers with complete fertilizer.

What other aspects do you consider when buying a plant for you garden? Do you shop for a specific brand of plant or seed?

_____

_____

_____

_____

_____

_____

_____

_____

_____

_____

_____

_____

_____

Spring Tip: Forsythia is a great shrub for hillsides. The tips of its branches take root when they reach the ground controlling erosion.

*D*o you have a garden helper? If so, who, and how did that person become your helper? _____

_____

_____

_____

_____

_____

_____

_____

_____

_____

_____

_____

_____

_____

_____

_____

_____

Spring Tip: Pansies are excellent plants for unpredictable spring weather. They liven up your faded garden when nothig else can, even when temperatures dip into the 20's.

Do you try to attract wildlife to your garden? If so, how?

_____

_____

_____

_____

_____

_____

_____

_____

_____

_____

_____

_____

_____

_____

_____

_____

_____

Spring Tip: Provide building materials for nesting birds. Fill a berry basket or a netting bag with pieces of string, dried grass, pet hair and twigs. Then hang it in a tree for accessibility.

$\mathcal{D}$o you have a compost pile? What kind is it and what do you put in it?

_____
_____
_____
_____
_____
_____
_____
_____
_____
_____
_____
_____
_____
_____
_____
_____
_____

Spring Tip: Chipped-bark mulch robs planting beds of nitrogen as it breaks down. Compost it for a year before using it in your bed.

Summer

Season of mists and mellow fruitfulness,
 Close bosom-friend of the maturing sun;
Conspiring with him how to load and bless
 With fruit the vines that round the thatch-eves run;
To bend with apples the moss'd cottage-trees,
 And fill all fruit with ripeness to the core;
 To swell the gourd, and plump the hazel shells
With a sweet kernel; to set budding more,
 And still more, later flowers for the bees,
 Until they think warm days will never cease,
 For Summer has o'er-brimm'd their clammy cells.

--*To Autumn*
by John Keats

What makes your garden special?

_____

_____

_____

_____

_____

_____

_____

_____

_____

_____

_____

_____

_____

_____

_____

_____

_____

Summer Tip: While your spring garden is still fresh in your mind, order spring-blooming bulbs to be certain of getting the best selection for next year.

$\mathcal{D}$o you belong to a garden club?

_____

_____

_____

_____

_____

_____

_____

_____

_____

_____

_____

_____

_____

_____

_____

_____

_____

_____

Summer Tip: Get your kids excited about composting by using a worm composting bin.

What time of day do you most enjoy spending in your garden? Why?

_____

_____

_____

_____

_____

_____

_____

_____

_____

_____

_____

_____

_____

_____

Summer Tip: Hanging baskets and containers need daily watering in hot weather. Metal, plastic, and wooden containers require the most attention.

What is the rarest item in your garden?

_____

_____

_____

_____

_____

_____

_____

_____

_____

_____

_____

_____

_____

_____

_____

_____

_____

Summer Tip: Turn late summer garden harvest and fall leaf piles into nutrient-rich soil amendments by creating a compost pile.

Have you planned or held any special events in your garden? If so, describe it.

_____

_____

_____

_____

_____

_____

_____

_____

_____

_____

_____

_____

_____

_____

_____

_____

_____

Summer Tip: Combat algae in your water garden by introducing snails and tadpoles, both of which will eat the algae.

How do you keep pets or wildlife from damaging plants in your garden?

_____

_____

_____

_____

_____

_____

_____

_____

_____

_____

_____

_____

_____

_____

_____

_____

Summer Tip: Deadhead your roses and prune out straggly, dead, and diseased canes. Clip suckers at the root by digging into the soil a bit.

What is the most prolific item in your garden?

_____

_____

_____

_____

_____

_____

_____

_____

_____

_____

_____

_____

_____

_____

_____

_____

Summer Tip: Hoe weeds and add them to the compost bin before they re-seed and cause problems next spring.

How do you control pests in your garden?

_____

_____

_____

_____

_____

_____

_____

_____

_____

_____

_____

_____

_____

_____

_____

_____

_____

Summer Tip: In the southern regions, you can start annual flower seeds in flats during the month of August in order to get transplant-size seedlings in September or October.

What plants would you like to add to your garden? Are there any that you wish to remove? _____

_____

_____

_____

_____

_____

_____

_____

_____

_____

_____

_____

_____

_____

_____

_____

Summer Tip: Prune cane berries after harvesting.

Do you name your indoor plants?

Summer Tip: Trimming faded flowers and pinching back annuals will stretch their bloom season.

*D*o you sing or talk to your plants? If so, what benefits do you see from it?

_____

_____

_____

_____

_____

_____

_____

_____

_____

_____

_____

_____

_____

_____

_____

_____

_____

_____

Summer Tip: Keep your lawn healthy by providing an inch of water weekly. Check by placing a can in the sprinkler's path and measure the collected water.

Name one thing about your garden that puzzles you. _____

_____

_____

_____

_____

_____

_____

_____

_____

_____

_____

_____

_____

_____

_____

_____

_____

Summer Tip: Mow your grass higher in order to keep the roots cool. Cut off about a third of the grass or less each time you mow.

*D*o you share your gardening talent in any special way with your friends, neighbors, or community?

_____

_____

_____

_____

_____

_____

_____

_____

_____

_____

_____

_____

_____

_____

_____

_____

_____

Summer Tip: Because container plants can dry out in a day, be sure to make arrangements for watering them if you go on vacation.

Do you ever take produce to a market to sell?

_____

_____

_____

_____

_____

_____

_____

_____

_____

_____

_____

_____

_____

_____

_____

_____

_____

Summer Tip: Get kids excited about gardening. Have them plant their own "zoo" with plants such as lamb's-ear, tiger lily, butterfly bush, and zebra grass.

Name one tool that you could never live without. Why?

_____

_____

_____

_____

_____

_____

_____

_____

_____

_____

_____

_____

_____

_____

_____

_____

Summer Tip: To remove dirt and to condition the metal, plunge small garden tools into a bucket filled with sand and motor oil.

When you are looking for gardening ideas and advice where do you search?

_____

_____

_____

_____

_____

_____

_____

_____

_____

_____

_____

_____

_____

_____

Summer Tip: A drip system is a great way of getting water to all your container plants.

Do you listen to music in your garden? If so, what kind? How does it affect you?

_____

_____

_____

_____

_____

_____

_____

_____

_____

_____

_____

_____

_____

_____

_____

_____

Summer Tip: Weeding is easiest when the soil is damp. Pull weeds by hand and remove the entire root.

What textures do you notice in your garden?

_____

_____

_____

_____

_____

_____

_____

_____

_____

_____

_____

_____

_____

_____

_____

_____

_____

_____

_____

Summer Tip: Harvest herbs just before the plant begins to flower in order for them to taste their best.

*I*s your climate dry, wet, or somewhere in between? How do you deal with this aspect of gardening?_____

_____

_____

_____

_____

_____

_____

_____

_____

_____

_____

_____

_____

_____

_____

_____

Summer Tip: Water sources, such as a bird bath, entice wildlife into your garden because they offer a place to drink and bathe.

Do you have a favorite ornament in your garden? When did you get it?

_____

_____

_____

_____

_____

_____

_____

_____

_____

_____

_____

_____

_____

_____

_____

_____

Summer Tip: Use 2- or 3-inches of mulch to conserve moisture and cut down on weeds around flowers, vegetables, ground covers, and young shrubs.

_D_o you have a favorite place to sit in your garden? What makes it your favorite?

_____

_____

_____

_____

_____

_____

_____

_____

_____

_____

_____

_____

_____

_____

_____

_____

_____

Summer Tip: Deter slugs by spreading crushed egg shells on the ground. They cut the slugs' bodies.

Autumn

Down every day in the solitude of the creek.
A serene autumn sun and westerly breeze
today as I sit here, the water surface
prettily moving in wind-ripples before me.
On a stout old beech at the edge, decayed
and slanting, almost fallen to the stream,
yet with life and leaves in its mossy limbs,
a gray squirrel, exploring, runs up and
down, flirts his tail, leaps to the ground,
sits on his haunches upright as he sees
me, (a Darwinian hint?) and then races
up the tree again.

--*Autumn Side-Bits*
by Walt Whitman

What was your biggest weed? What steps have you taken to remove it?

_____

_____

_____

_____

_____

_____

_____

_____

_____

_____

_____

_____

_____

_____

_____

_____

_____

Autumn Tip: Divide peonies, irises, and daylilies in August after plants have finished blooming and while they are resting. Replant some and share some with a gardening friend.

*D*id you plant anything in your garden that you now wish you hadn't? If so, what?

_____

_____

_____

_____

_____

_____

_____

_____

_____

_____

_____

_____

_____

_____

_____

_____

_____

Autumn Tip: Plant garlic in the fall for an early summer harvest.

What bulbs, if any, are you planting for next spring?

_____

_____

_____

_____

_____

_____

_____

_____

_____

_____

_____

_____

_____

_____

_____

_____

_____

Autumn Tip: After an early harvest, plant a second garden of cool-season vegetables like carrots, lettuce, and broccoli to harvest in fall and early winter.

What was your greatest gardening success? Why do you consider it your greatest?

_____

_____

_____

_____

_____

_____

_____

_____

_____

_____

_____

_____

_____

_____

_____

_____

_____

_____

_____

Autumn Tip: To prepare beds for the fall planting season, dig at least 10 to 12 inches deep mixing in a 2- to 3-inch layer of organic matter.

What was your worst gardening failure? What will you do differently in the future?

_____

_____

_____

_____

_____

_____

_____

_____

_____

_____

_____

_____

_____

_____

_____

_____

_____

Autumn Tip: Warm soil temps and cooler days make for ideal planting conditions. Try ornamental cabbage and fall-blooming flowers to add color to your fading landscape.

When do you begin harvesting the fruit of all your hard work?

_____

_____

_____

_____

_____

_____

_____

_____

_____

_____

_____

_____

_____

_____

_____

_____

Autumn Tip: As the last of your perennials finish blooming, begin fall clean-up, but save plants that have interesting seedpods or foliage to add interest to your winter garden.

What do you do with the harvest?

_____

_____

_____

_____

_____

_____

_____

_____

_____

_____

_____

_____

_____

_____

_____

_____

_____

_____

_____

_____

Autumn Tip: If you are expecting frost, cover summer vegetables with plastic, but be sure to uncover them before the sun comes out the next day.

What was the biggest obstacle to getting your garden to grow as you desired? How did you overcome it?

_____

_____

_____

_____

_____

_____

_____

_____

_____

_____

_____

_____

_____

_____

_____

_____

_____

Autumn Tip: In areas where moisture or bulb-rot is a problem, create raised beds or infill bulb-holes with coarse builder's sand to encourage drainage.

What would you say is the secret to a successful garden? _____

_____

_____

_____

_____

_____

_____

_____

_____

_____

_____

_____

_____

_____

_____

_____

_____

_____

Autumn Tip: If you are looking for good cover crop companions, try winter wheat or barley or any of the winter greens.

On average, how much time do you spend each week in your garden?

_____

_____

_____

_____

_____

_____

_____

_____

_____

_____

_____

_____

_____

_____

Autumn Tip: You can still plant bulbs in October if the ground is not yet frozen. Almost any bulb other than Narcissus can be planted in late autumn.

If you could change one thing about your garden, what would it be?_____

_____

_____

_____

_____

_____

_____

_____

_____

_____

_____

_____

_____

_____

_____

_____

Autumn Tip: Harvest pumpkins and gourds before frost.

What benefits both tangible and intangible do you gain from gardening?

_____

_____

_____

_____

_____

_____

_____

_____

_____

_____

_____

_____

_____

_____

_____

_____

_____

Autumn Tip: Wrap tree trunks in the fall to help them withstand the stresses of sudden temperature changes, windburn, and sunscald.

How do you incorporate your garden into your home? _____

_____

_____

_____

_____

_____

_____

_____

_____

_____

_____

_____

_____

_____

_____

_____

Autumn Tip: Fall and spring are the best time to transplant trees because they are dormant and require little food and water during dormancy.

What bulbs, if any, have you dug up in order to store them for the coming winter months?_____

_____

_____

_____

_____

_____

_____

_____

_____

_____

_____

_____

_____

_____

_____

_____

_____

Autumn Tip: Decaying leaves release toxins that kill fish. Place plastic netting over the surface of your fishpond to prohibit falling leaves from entering.

What do you like most about your garden? What do you like least about it?

_____

_____

_____

_____

_____

_____

_____

_____

_____

_____

_____

_____

_____

_____

_____

_____

_____

_____

Autumn Tip: Use your lawn mower to mulch the last layer of leaves in the fall.

What is your best kept secret concerning gardening?

_____

_____

_____

_____

_____

_____

_____

_____

_____

_____

_____

_____

_____

_____

_____

Autumn Tip: Clean containers after using them all summer. Scrub the inside with a wire brush, and then disinfect them using a 10% bleach solution. Rinse them well and store.

D
o you notice any migration patterns that have brought special guest to your garden in the fall?_____

_____

_____

_____

_____

_____

_____

_____

_____

_____

_____

_____

_____

_____

Autumn Tip: Don't throw away those lawn clippings in the fall. Put them in your compost pile along with your shredded leaves in order to add them to the soil in the spring.

Desbribe your first attempts at gardening. What did you learn from it? _____

_____

_____

_____

_____

_____

_____

_____

_____

_____

_____

_____

_____

_____

_____

_____

Autumn Tip: Stop fertilizing roses at least two months before freezing temperatures arrive to prevent late growth that is damaged by falling temperatures.

How do you feel as you get your garden ready for the coming cold weather?

_____

_____

_____

_____

_____

_____

_____

_____

_____

_____

_____

_____

_____

_____

Autumn Tip: Insulate your compost pile with a foot or so of hay or straw when the temperature falls. It decomposes and can be turned into the pile in early spring.

Do you use any items from your garden during the celebration of fall holidays?

_____

_____

_____

_____

_____

_____

_____

_____

_____

_____

_____

_____

_____

_____

_____

_____

_____

Autumn Tip: Tropical plants from your water garden or other plants that won't survive the winter can be tossed into the compost pile.

*H*ow do you dispose of all the leaves that fall into your garden? _____

_____

_____

_____

_____

_____

_____

_____

_____

_____

_____

_____

_____

_____

_____

_____

_____

Autumn Tip: Keep a bag of dry autumn leaves to add to your compost pile in the summer when you may lack dry material and are overwhelmed with moist green materials.

Plantings

List the plants you have grown during your gardening career. Check whether they have been successful or unsuccesful attempts.

_____	☐ Successful	☐ Unsuccessful
_____	☐ Successful	☐ Unsuccessful
_____	☐ Successful	☐ Unsuccessful
_____	☐ Successful	☐ Unsuccessful
_____	☐ Successful	☐ Unsuccessful
_____	☐ Successful	☐ Unsuccessful
_____	☐ Successful	☐ Unsuccessful
_____	☐ Successful	☐ Unsuccessful
_____	☐ Successful	☐ Unsuccessful
_____	☐ Successful	☐ Unsuccessful
_____	☐ Successful	☐ Unsuccessful
_____	☐ Successful	☐ Unsuccessful
_____	☐ Successful	☐ Unsuccessful
_____	☐ Successful	☐ Unsuccessful
_____	☐ Successful	☐ Unsuccessful
_____	☐ Successful	☐ Unsuccessful
_____	☐ Successful	☐ Unsuccessful
_____	☐ Successful	☐ Unsuccessful

_____	☐ Successful	☐ Unsuccessful
_____	☐ Successful	☐ Unsuccessful
_____	☐ Successful	☐ Unsuccessful
_____	☐ Successful	☐ Unsuccessful
_____	☐ Successful	☐ Unsuccessful
_____	☐ Successful	☐ Unsuccessful
_____	☐ Successful	☐ Unsuccessful
_____	☐ Successful	☐ Unsuccessful
_____	☐ Successful	☐ Unsuccessful
_____	☐ Successful	☐ Unsuccessful
_____	☐ Successful	☐ Unsuccessful
_____	☐ Successful	☐ Unsuccessful
_____	☐ Successful	☐ Unsuccessful
_____	☐ Successful	☐ Unsuccessful
_____	☐ Successful	☐ Unsuccessful
_____	☐ Successful	☐ Unsuccessful
_____	☐ Successful	☐ Unsuccessful
_____	☐ Successful	☐ Unsuccessful
_____	☐ Successful	☐ Unsuccessful
_____	☐ Successful	☐ Unsuccessful
_____	☐ Successful	☐ Unsuccessful
_____	☐ Successful	☐ Unsuccessful
_____	☐ Successful	☐ Unsuccessful
_____	☐ Successful	☐ Unsuccessful

Notes

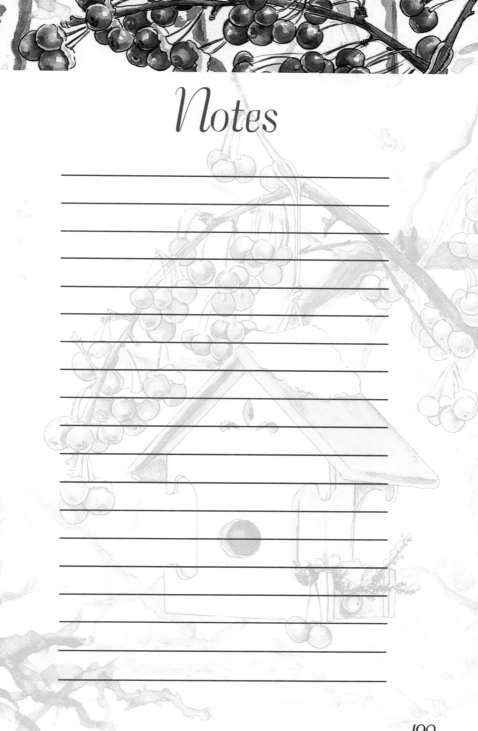

Notes

_____

_____

_____

_____

_____

_____

_____

_____

_____

_____

_____

_____

_____

_____

_____

_____

Photos

Photos

Photos